THE GREEN LLAMA

Welcome to Planet 23

Green Llama LLC

Chicago, IL

www.greenllama.org

Concept by **Xavier "OSKE" Hernandez**
Story by **Lonnie Edwards**
Illustration by **Hiram "TEEL ONE" Villa**
Produced by **Anthony Garritano**

Round Table Companies

www.roundtablecompanies.com

Design, layout, and production support by **Sunny DiMartino**

Editorial support by **Keli McNeill, Sunny DiMartino**
Adrian Bumgarner, Sheila Harris

. . . .

First Edition: April 2023

10 9 8 7 6 5 4 3 2 1

ISBN Paperback: 979-8-9879246-0-0

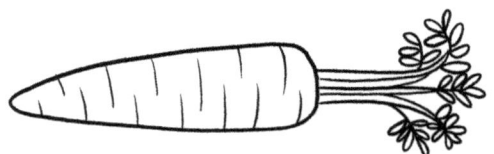

CHAPTER ONE

Hi, My Name Is . . .

In a galaxy far, far away, beyond many planets and stars, there was a place called PLANET 23. With clear skies, forests filled with giant broccoli trees, and strawberries the size of boulders, Planet 23 was a place that happy, whimsical creatures called home.

Everyone is excited because today is a special day. A new student is arriving at school.

"If we can have the Green Llama meet the new student in the office and bring them back to class, that would be wonderful," says Mrs. Middlebrooks.

The Green Llama walks excitedly down the hallway to the office to meet the new student.

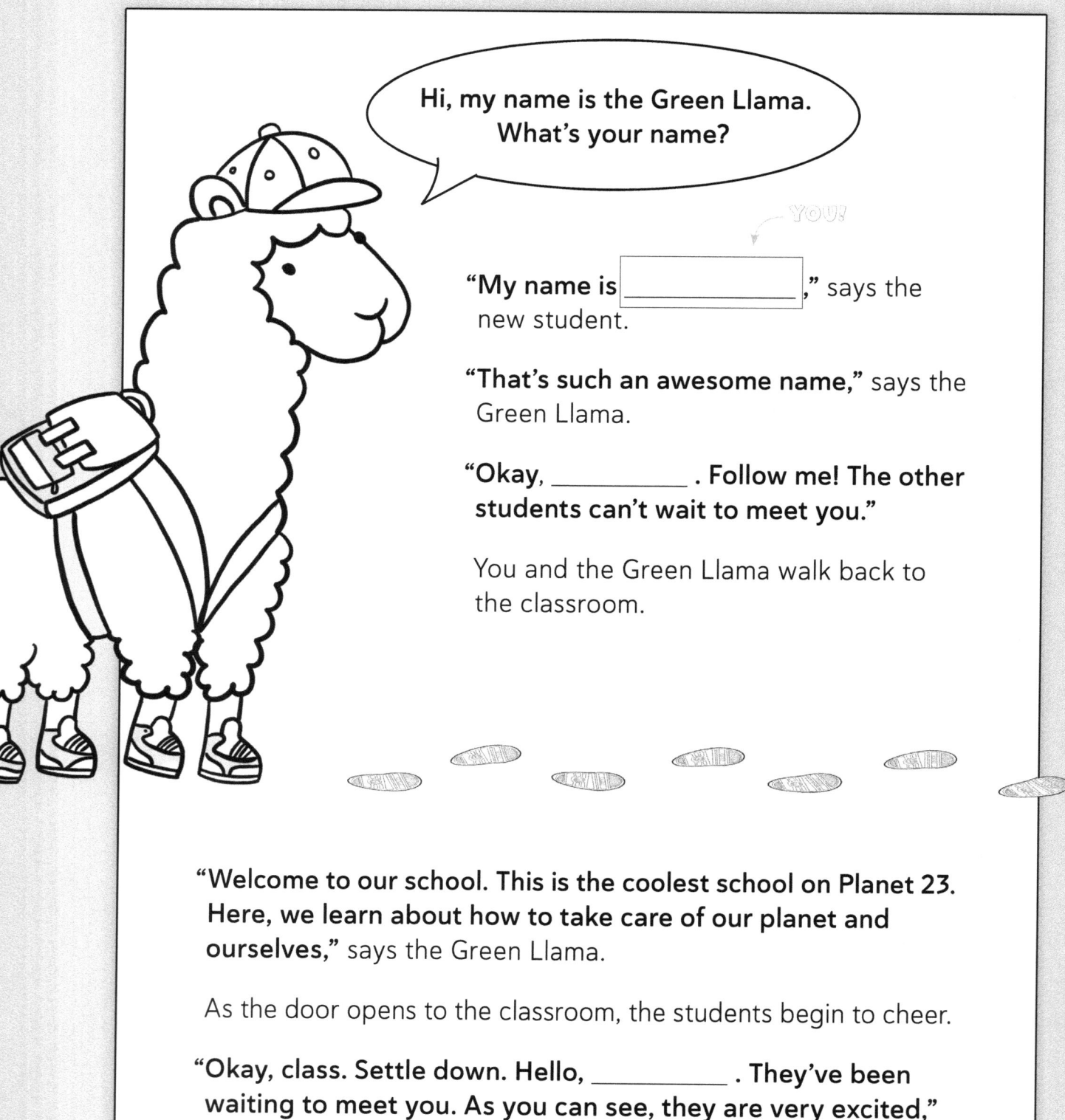

Hi, my name is the Green Llama. What's your name?

YOU!

"My name is _____," says the new student.

"That's such an awesome name," says the Green Llama.

"Okay, _____ . Follow me! The other students can't wait to meet you."

You and the Green Llama walk back to the classroom.

"Welcome to our school. This is the coolest school on Planet 23. Here, we learn about how to take care of our planet and ourselves," says the Green Llama.

As the door opens to the classroom, the students begin to cheer.

"Okay, class. Settle down. Hello, _____ . They've been waiting to meet you. As you can see, they are very excited," says Mrs. Middlebrooks.

"Thank you, Green Llama. You can have a seat now."

"Please tell the class about yourself." You stand in front of the class and take a deep breath. Mrs. Middlebrooks does her best to encourage you.

"Don't be nervous. Take your time. I have a few questions to get you started . . ."

1 Where are you from?

2 How old are you?

3 What are your favorite games to play?

4 What are your favorite things to eat?

✒ Answer the questions using a complete sentence.

✎ What do you like to do for fun? Circle and color in all your favorite activities. Draw a picture of something you like to do that isn't pictured.

Draw a picture of you and the llama in the space below.

"Great job! You can sit down now, thank you. Okay, class. We have a few minutes before lunch. If _____ can answer this question correctly, everyone will get recess after lunch."

All of the students look at you with excitement.
"Good luck. We're all counting on you!"
Mrs. Middlebrooks says.

☑ Can you circle and color in *only* the fruits and vegetables?

"That was very impressive, _____ . Time for lunch . . . and recess!"

Everyone in the classroom cheers.

ALL ABOUT YOU

What are your favorite fruits and vegetables?

_____

_____

Do you know where fruits and vegetables come from?

_____

_____

THINK ABOUT THE STORY

What kinds of games will you and the llama play outside during recess?

_____

_____

Do you think you and the llama will become friends?

_____

_____

ACTIVITY

Track what you eat. List all the fruits and vegetables you eat over the next week.

Day 1	Day 2	Day 3	Day 4

Day 5	Day 6	Day 7

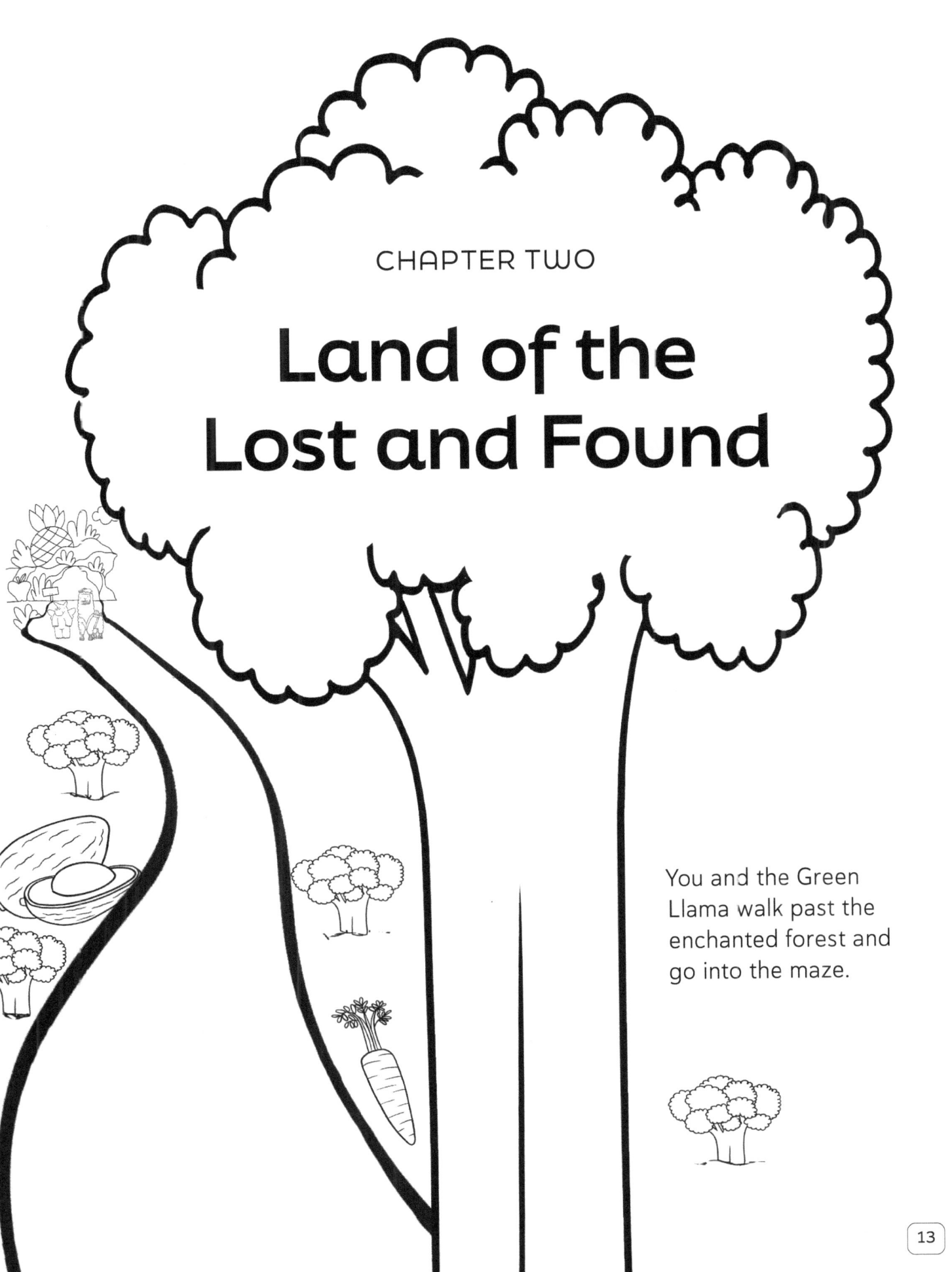

CHAPTER TWO

Land of the Lost and Found

You and the Green Llama walk past the enchanted forest and go into the maze.

"Don't go too far! It's easy to get lost in the mazes," says Mrs. Middlebrooks.

You and the Green Llama walk outside.

"The mazes aren't so bad," the Green Llama says. **"They have the best fruits and vegetables inside!"**

Color in the picture using the number key.

1: Gray

2: Brown

3: Red

4: Green

5: Black

6: Yellow

7: Purple

8: Dark Green

9: Orange

10: White

The Green Llama smiles at you and says, **"I know these mazes like the back of my neck! Try to keep up, though, because I move fast!"**

You zip and dash through the maze, turning every corner.

Suddenly, the Green Llama stops and looks up. **"This is glorious! Help me pick all the fruits and vegetables to fill up my backpack. Then we can share with the entire class!"**

_____

✎ Solve the word problems below. Be sure to draw out your equation! Draw a picture to help you find the answer. Write the number in the box and spell it on the line provided.

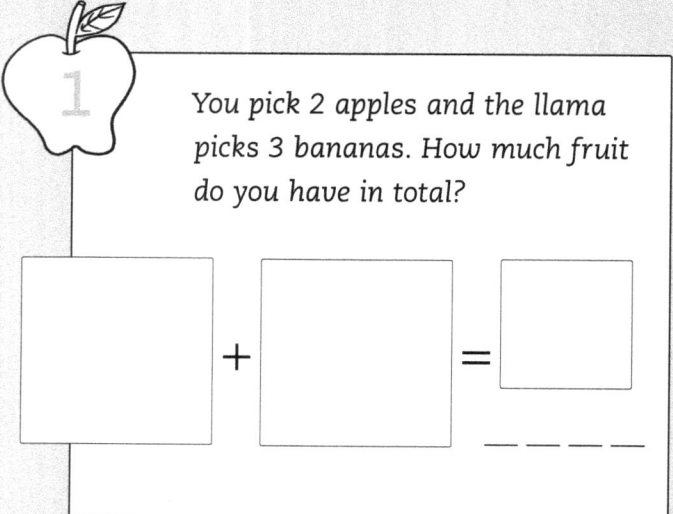

You pick 2 apples and the llama picks 3 bananas. How much fruit do you have in total?

☐ + ☐ = ☐
_ _ _ _ _

You find 4 tomatoes and the llama finds 3 tomatoes. How many more tomatoes did you find than the llama?

☐ − ☐ = ☐
_ _ _

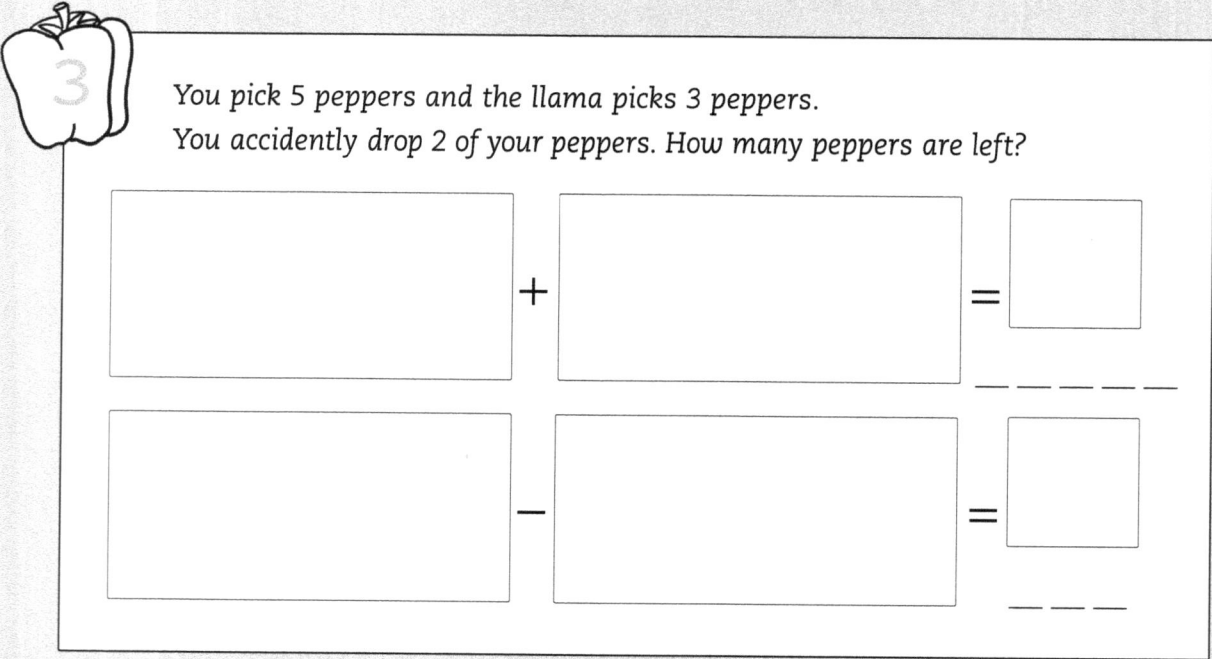

You pick 5 peppers and the llama picks 3 peppers. You accidently drop 2 of your peppers. How many peppers are left?

☐ + ☐ = ☐
_ _ _ _ _

☐ − ☐ = ☐
_ _ _

As you are helping the Green Llama put fruits and vegetables into his backpack, you see a flash of light and hear a loud crash. The Green Llama turns to you and says, **"Did you see that? Did you hear that? What if it's aliens?"**

ALL ABOUT YOU

What are foods you like to eat that are made with tomatoes?

_____

_____

Some peppers are spicy. What does food taste like when it is spicy? Do you like spicy foods?

_____

THINK ABOUT THE STORY

You and the llama heard a loud noise and there were sparks of bright light when you were in the garden. What do you think that was? What do you think will happen next?

_____

_____

_____

_____

ACTIVITY

Please search about how plants grow. Can you list all the stages in a plant's growth? Can you list all the different parts of a plant? Draw a plant and label its parts.

*Meanwhile,
far, far away . . .*

CHAPTER THREE

Meet Captain Atlas

"**Five . . . four . . . three . . . two . . . one . . . liftoff!**" Captain Atlas looks over at M.A.T. and says, "**Our journey begins. I hope you're ready!**" The spaceship flies through the sky like a shooting star floating through the solar system. Each day that passes, M.A.T. makes sure to keep Captain Atlas's brain in peak condition by working on problem-solving.

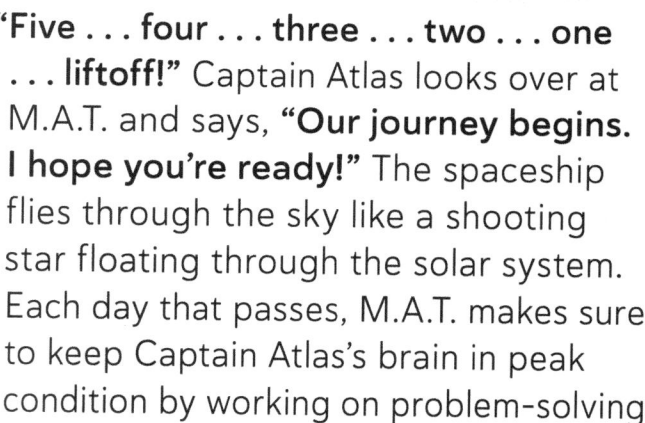

✏️ Help Captain Atlas operate the spaceship by decoding the objects into letters to spell out the words.

KEY

The captain's ship gets farther and farther from Earth. On their journey, the captain experiences so many amazing adventures on different planets while traveling from galaxy to galaxy.

✎ Let's do some counting and writing!
Write the number and write out the word.

*Count all the **stars** in the picture.* → | | |
|---|---|

*Next, count the number of **planets** in the picture.* → | | |
|---|---|

*Next, count the number of **satellites** in the picture.* → | | |
|---|---|

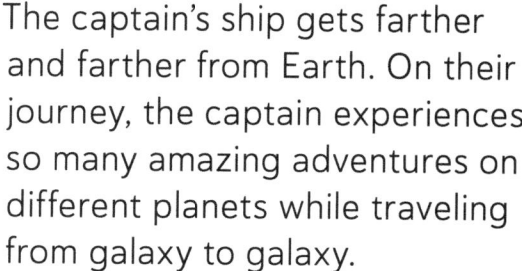

One day as Captain Atlas is studying, there is a loud noise. M.A.T. comes running in, shouting, **"Captain Atlas, we seem to be flying through a meteor shower. If the ship continues to take damage, I'm not sure if REP-1 and C3-1 can repair the damage quickly enough. We seem to be losing fuel rapidly. I think we should find the closest planet for an emergency landing."**

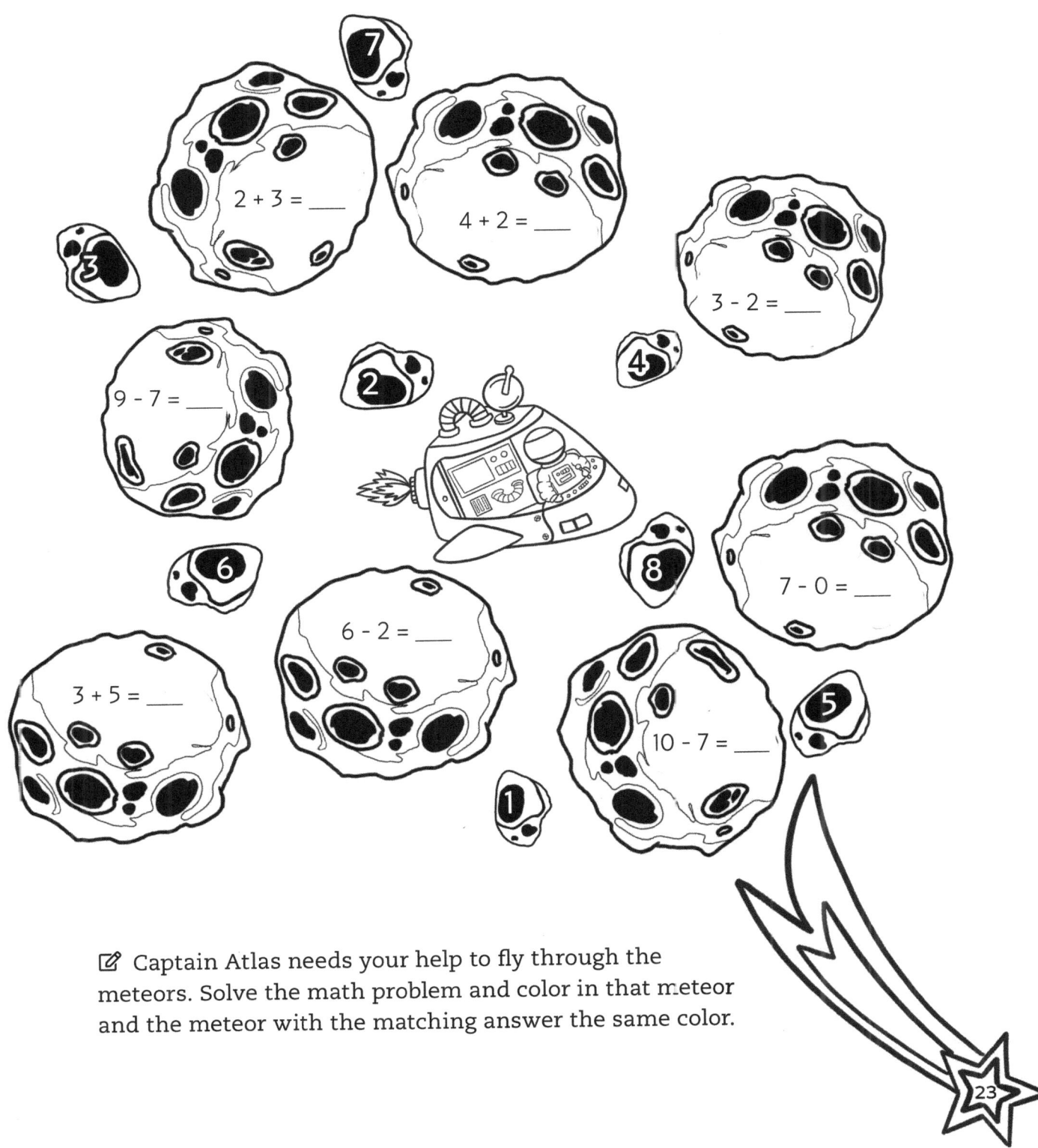

☑ Captain Atlas needs your help to fly through the meteors. Solve the math problem and color in that meteor and the meteor with the matching answer the same color.

23

"Everyone, prepare for emergency landing! M.A.T., can you give me the coordinates of the nearest planet we can safely land on in search of fuel and any other resources?" says Captain Atlas.

"One moment." M.A.T. scans the map in front of him.

✍ Help M.A.T. with his digital scans by solving the math problems below.

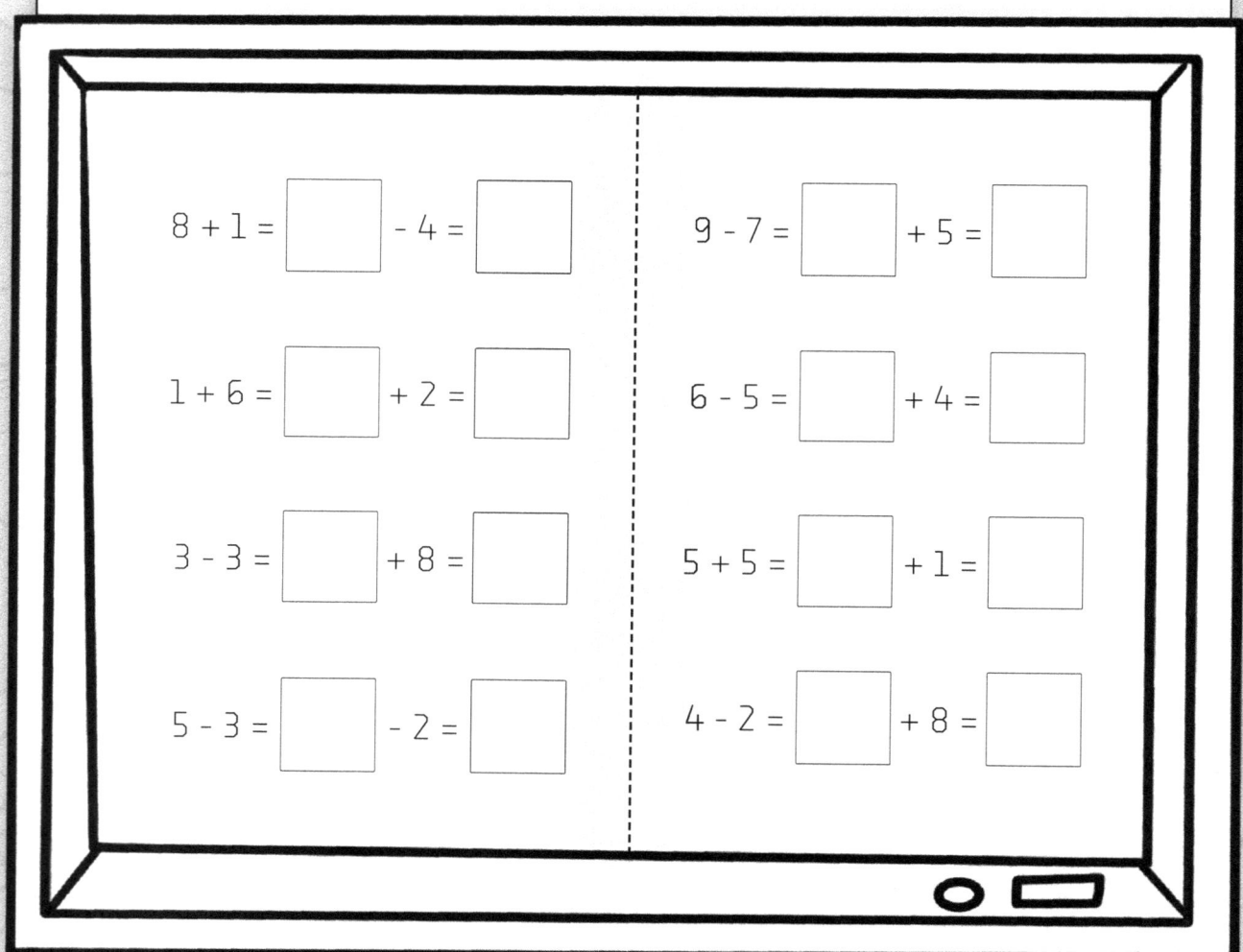

$8 + 1 =$ ☐ $- 4 =$ ☐ $9 - 7 =$ ☐ $+ 5 =$ ☐

$1 + 6 =$ ☐ $+ 2 =$ ☐ $6 - 5 =$ ☐ $+ 4 =$ ☐

$3 - 3 =$ ☐ $+ 8 =$ ☐ $5 + 5 =$ ☐ $+ 1 =$ ☐

$5 - 3 =$ ☐ $- 2 =$ ☐ $4 - 2 =$ ☐ $+ 8 =$ ☐

Way to go! You helped him find a place to land!

"There seems to be a place called 'Planet 23' not far away. It is populated though, so we must proceed with caution."

Captain Atlas looks at the image of Planet 23 that M.A.T. has projected.

"Everyone, prepare for landing. Planet 23, here we come!"

✎ Prepare the spaceship for the emergency landing by identifying the differences in the two pictures of Captain Atlas. Circle all of the differences you can see between the two pictures.

ALL ABOUT YOU

Captain Atlas is an astronaut. Do you know what an astronaut does? Would you like to be an astronaut when you grow up? Why or why not?

_____

_____

What are some things you would need to know to be able to fly a spaceship?

_____

_____

THINK ABOUT THE STORY

Why were REP-1 and C3-1 worried about the meteor shower? What could happen to the ship when flying through a meteor shower?

_____

_____

What do you think Planet 23 will look like when Captain Atlas lands?

_____

_____

ACTIVITY

Do you know the names of the first astronauts? Where did they go in their spaceship?

Can you find and watch a video of the first time astronauts landed somewhere other than Earth?

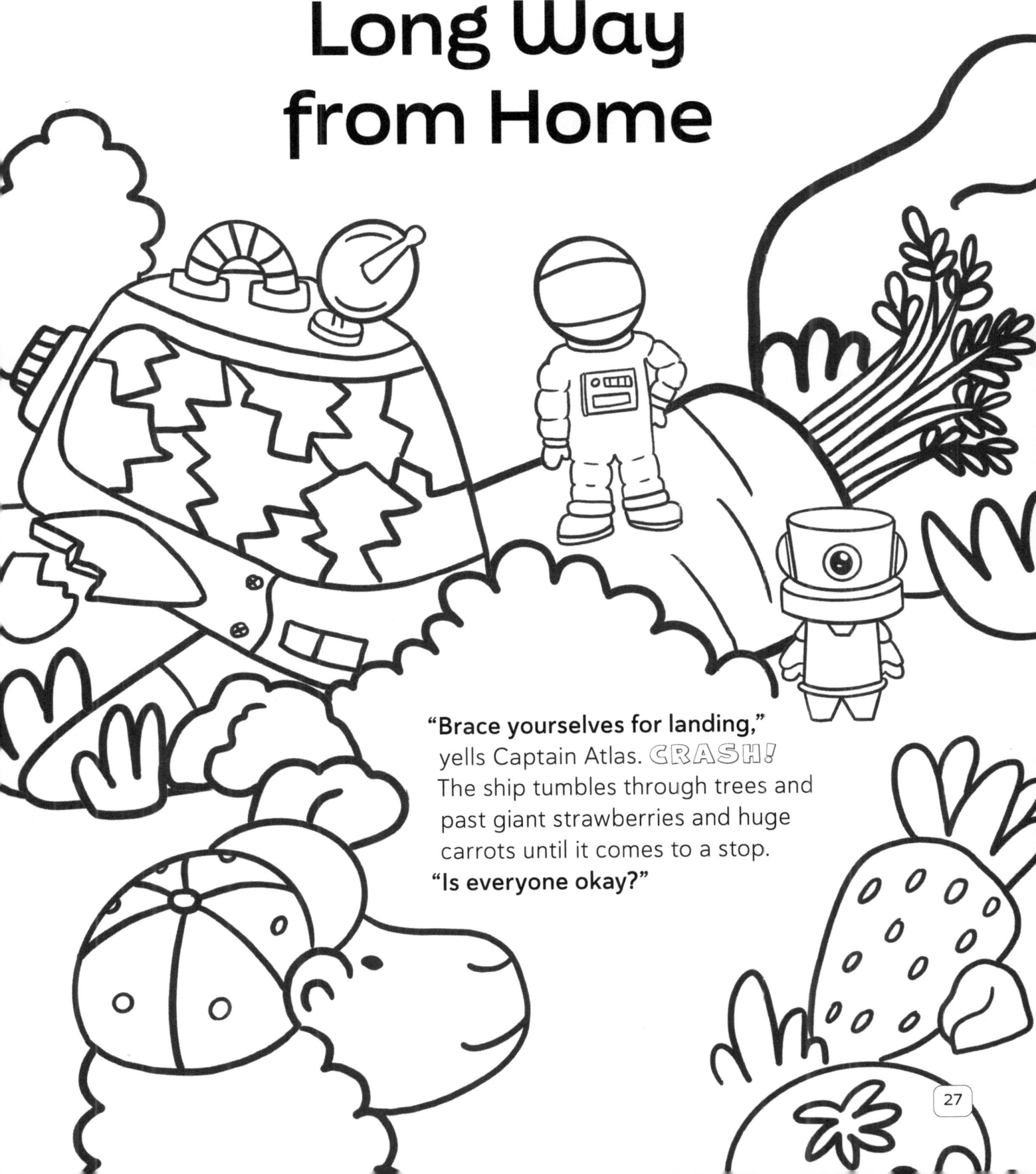

CHAPTER FOUR

Long Way from Home

"Brace yourselves for landing," yells Captain Atlas. CRASH! The ship tumbles through trees and past giant strawberries and huge carrots until it comes to a stop. "Is everyone okay?"

Captain Atlas, C3-1, REP-1, and M.A.T. exit the spaceship.
"C3-1, it looks like this ship is going to need a lot of work. Can you and REP-1 start repairing the damage? I'm going to take a look around."

The captain starts to explore the forest and looks around in amazement. **"I've never seen anything like this."**

✎ Help to explore Planet 23 by completing the word search.

See if you can find the words on the list!

```
L  R  X  U  A  R  Y
A  S  T  A  R  S  P
N  F  E  C  A  H  U
D  V  C  E  R  H  M
I  R  R  R  O  E  E
N  N  A  K  B  W  T
G  U  S  M  O  A  E
P  O  H  N  T  Z  O
A  T  L  A  S  R  R
U  W  V  E  E  T  K
T  S  U  R  E  F  Z
X  A  D  T  F  N  U
J  O  U  R  N  E  Y
V  P  S  S  Y  A  L
Y  L  R  W  W  R  S
T  A  Z  Z  O  T  E
T  N  U  I  S  H  T
O  E  E  F  A  L  Q
P  T  V  G  Q  I  R
```

ATLAS

CRASH

EARTH

JOURNEY

LANDING

METEOR

PLANET

ROBOTS

STARS

Captain Atlas hears a noise from inside the forest.

"M.A.T., can you scan the area? I think I heard something,"
Captain Atlas says quietly.

You and the Green Llama slowly step backward into the forest.
The Green Llama steps on a branch, making a loud noise.
M.A.T. begins to move toward the sound. **"Scanning area.
Movement detected, Captain Atlas."**

✐ As M.A.T. begins to scan, it starts to recognize patterns.
Help M.A.T. identify the next object in each of the patterns.

    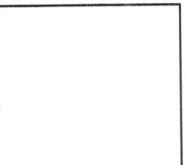

tomato	orange	orange	tomato	orange	

 broccoli  pepper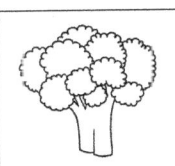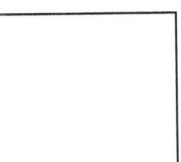

"Don't move! If we don't make any sudden movements, the aliens will give up and leave. I've seen it work in movies," whispers the Green Llama.

M.A.T. and Captain Atlas slowly begin to walk closer to where you and the Green Llama are hiding. **"It's okay. Don't be alarmed,"** says Captain Atlas.

 Figure out what Captain Atlas says next by solving the math problems and using the key.

4 + 2 = ___   1 + 2 = ___

2 + 2 = ___   3 + 4 = ___   3 - 1 = ___   5 - 2 = ___

1 + 0 = ___   3 + 2 = ___

2 - 2 = ___   4 - 1 = ___   2 + 6 = ___   3 + 1 = ___   6 - 3 = ___

The Green Llama looks at you and whispers, **"I think these aliens speak the same language we do. Maybe I should say hello?"**

_____

✍ There are over one million different languages spoken throughout the world today. How many can you list below? Circle the languages you know how to speak.

_____   _____

_____   _____

_____   _____

_____   _____

_____   _____

_____   _____

_____   _____

_____   _____

Out of the darkness, Captain Atlas sees a silhouette of you and the Green Llama hidden in the trees. Cautiously, you both step out and into the light to greet Captain Atlas. **"Hi. I'm the Green Llama, and this is my friend _____ . What's your name?"** says the Green Llama.

✏ Finish drawing the picture of M.A.T.

Captain Atlas looks at M.A.T. They are both speechless for a moment and stare in disbelief. **"Wait. You can talk? That is amazing! You're a green llama!"** Captain Atlas says.

✏️ Help Captain Atlas learn some new words by matching the word to its correct meaning. Then use the word in a sentence.

scan — big surprise

amazement — tastes good

alarmed — make power

sustainable — scared

fuel — look at all parts

delicious — made of renewable resources

scan _____

_____

amazement _____

_____

alarmed _____

_____

fuel _____

_____

sustainable _____

_____

delicious _____

_____

"Well, actually, I'm *THE* Green Llama, and everyone on Planet 23 can talk. Where are you from?" says the Green Llama.

Captain Atlas points to the sky. **"Have you heard of a place called Earth? That's where I'm from."**

The Green Llama looks at the sky and says, **"I've heard of planet Earth, but I only know a few things that I learned from my parents. Hey _____ , how much do you know about Earth?"**

✎ In the space below, list three to five facts that you know about Earth.

1 _____

_____

2 _____

_____

3 _____

_____

4 _____

_____

5 _____

_____

Can you name all the continents? Use the scrambled letters to spell the name of each continent shown on the map.

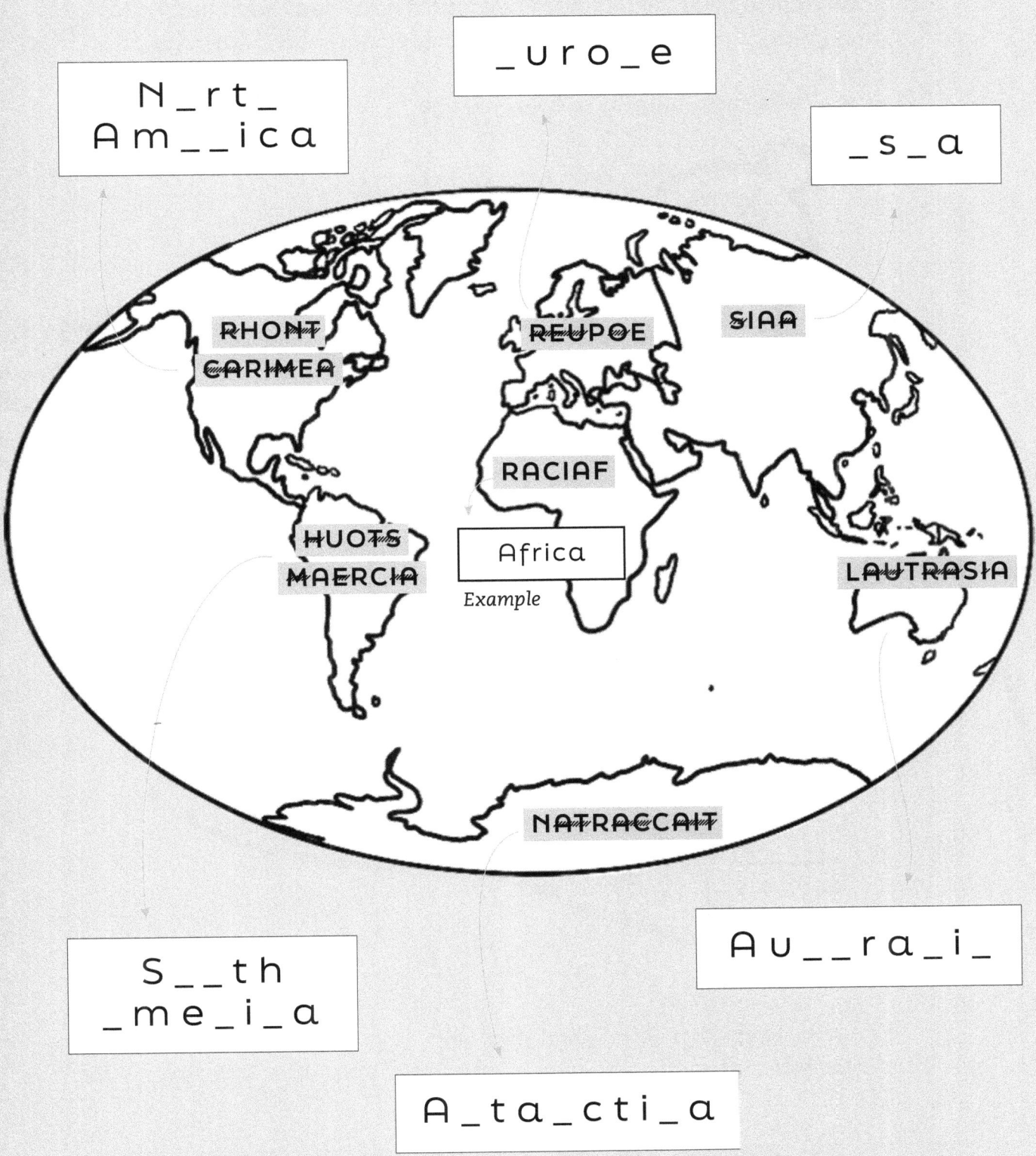

_ u r o _ e

N _ r t _
A m _ _ i c a

_ s _ a

RHONT
CARIMEA

REUPOE

SIAA

RACIAF

Africa
Example

HUOTS
MAERCIA

LAUTRASIA

NATRACCAIT

S _ _ t h
_ m e _ i _ a

A u _ _ r a _ i _

A _ t a _ c t i _ a

"**Wow! This looks like the spaceship my parents were on when they went into space to explore, except theirs was much larger . . . and cooler,**" the Green Llama says, pretending not to be amazed.

"**That makes sense. Llamas are very large,**" Captain Atlas says.

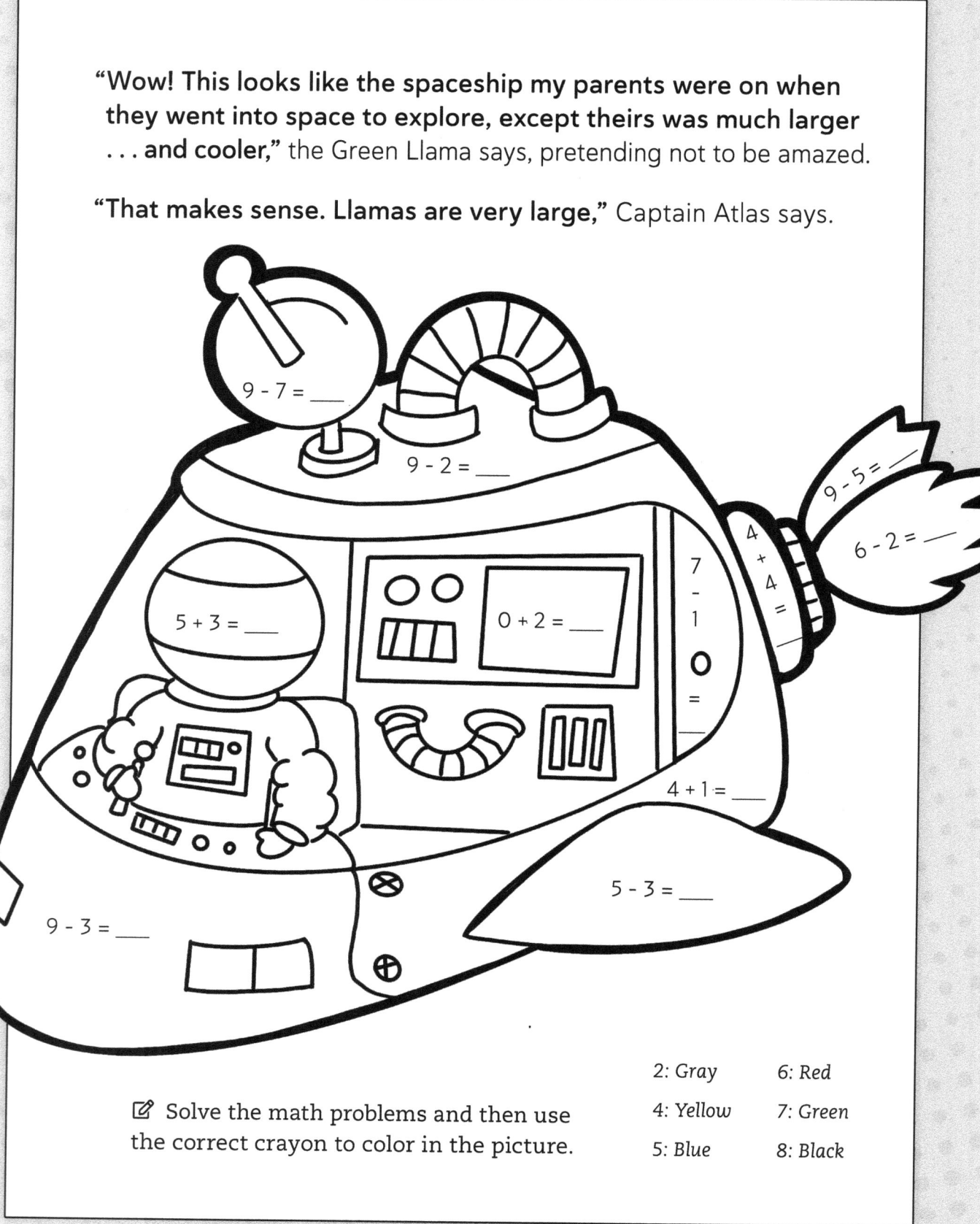

✐ Solve the math problems and then use the correct crayon to color in the picture.

2: Gray	6: Red
4: Yellow	7: Green
5: Blue	8: Black

"I wonder if you could help me. I need to figure out a plan to get me back home. My robots can fix our ship, but I need some help finding fuel. It's the only way we can get home," Captain Atlas responds.

_____

✍ Help the robots fix the ship by solving the math problems and identifying which number is larger and will provide more fuel! Circle or place a star next to the best option.

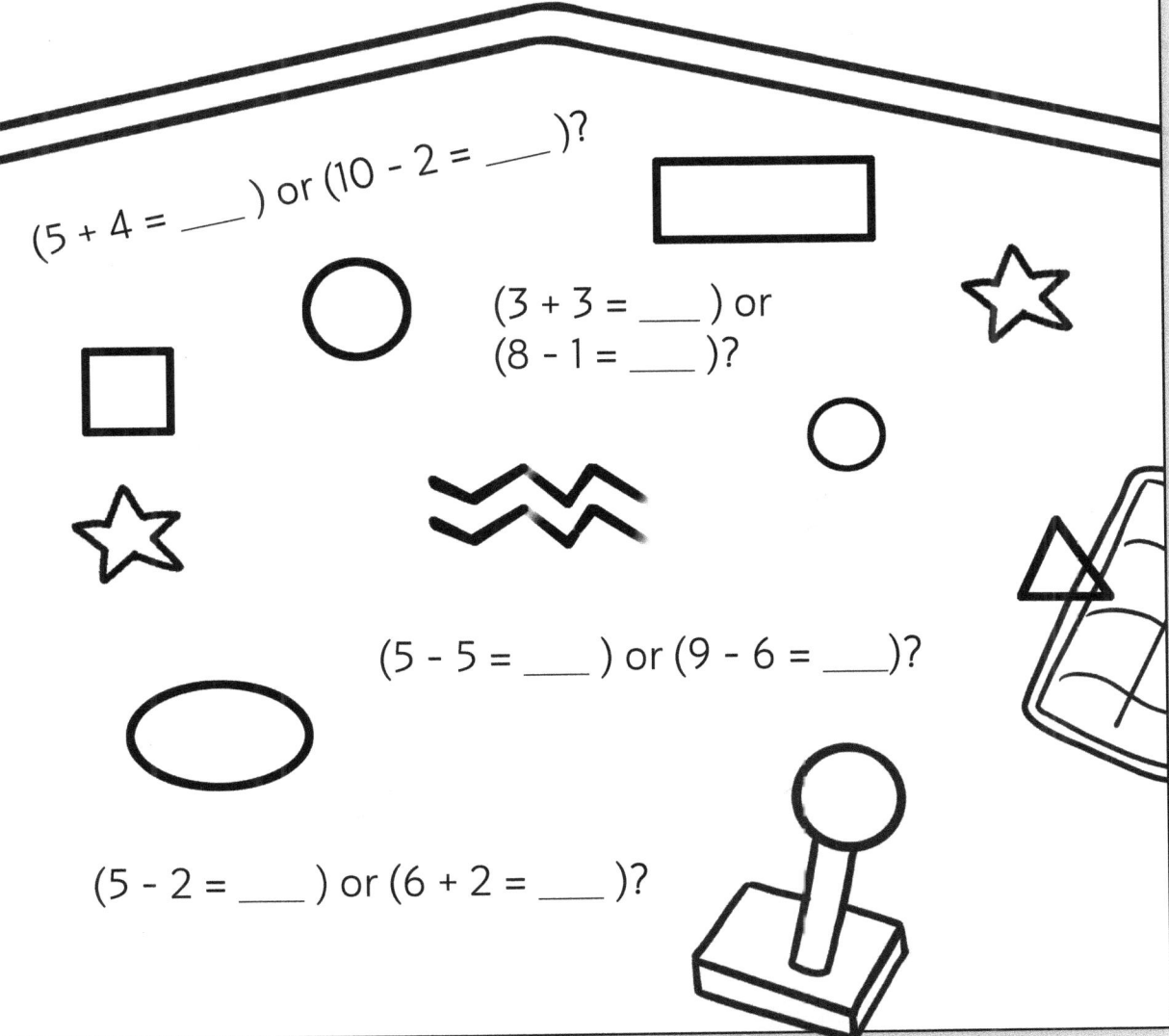

$(5 + 4 =$ ___$)$ or $(10 - 2 =$ ___$)$?

$(3 + 3 =$ ___$)$ or $(8 - 1 =$ ___$)$?

$(5 - 5 =$ ___$)$ or $(9 - 6 =$ ___$)$?

$(5 - 2 =$ ___$)$ or $(6 + 2 =$ ___$)$?

"Our planet has all types of sustainable fuel. We use fruits and vegetables for everything. Not only do they fuel us, but they also fuel our cars and provide heat for our homes. Plus, they are delicious to eat!" says the Green Llama.

_____

✎ Captain Atlas asks you to explain where all of these healthy foods come from. Use the remaining letters to spell out the word.

G R U C

A		R	I			L	T	U		E

✎ What does this word mean? Write the definition below.

_____

_____

_____

_____

_____

_____

_____

_____

Captain Atlas is very interested in learning more. You say that everything starts from a tiny seed.

✎ Using the words from the list below, label the parts of the plant.

seed　*leaves*　*stem*　*fruit*　*roots*

"This is so amazing!" Captain Atlas shouts. **"Where do you get your food from?"**

✎ Color in the pictures of the different places where you and your family get your food.

✎ You have learned so many things from the Green Llama and Captain Atlas. Fill in the correct words on the crossword puzzle below.

─ACROSS─

2. Some families get their _____ from farmer's markets.

4. You and the _____ Llama love going on adventures.

7. _____ Atlas flies the ship in outer space.

─DOWN─

1. The Green Llama's _____ is Planet 23.

3. The Green Llama and you have become _____ .

5. You should always eat _____ foods.

6. Captain Atlas comes from the planet _____ .

The Green Llama points in the direction of the school. **"We were going to give these fruits and vegetables to Mrs. Middlebrooks and our classmates, but maybe if we gather more, we can use it to fuel your ship. Let's head back to class and ask everyone for help."**

You, Captain Atlas, and the Green Llama begin to walk back through the enchanted forest and maze to go back to school.

✍ Color in the picture.

ALL ABOUT YOU

When things are broken, like Captain Atlas's spaceship, they need to be fixed. Can you name tools that you have seen or used before? How do they work? Who uses them?

_____

_____

_____

_____

THINK ABOUT THE STORY

What do you think will happen to Captain Atlas if you and the Green Llama do not find enough fuel for the spaceship? Could there be any other way Captain Atlas can get home?

_____

_____

Can you tell Captain Atlas about your first day at school and the names of different foods on Planet 23?

_____

_____

_____

_____

ACTIVITY

Rocket ships have been taking people to faraway places for a long time. Can you find pictures and/or videos of rocket ships? What makes rocket ships go so fast, and how fast can they go?

CHAPTER FIVE

Until We Meet Again

You all arrive back at the school. The Green Llama turns to speak to the group and says, **"Okay, we're a little late. I don't want to scare our classmates, because they've never seen an alien before. I will go in first, and I'm sure Mrs. Middlebrooks can help us figure out what to do next."**

45

THINK ABOUT THE STORY

What do you think will happen next? Read the questions below and discuss your thoughts.

1 How do you think the classmates will react to Captain Atlas?

2 Do you think Mrs. Middlebrooks will be concerned they were gone for so long? Why?

3 Do you like to meet new people? Why or why not?

4 When you first meet somebody new, what do you do?

5 Can you introduce yourself to the class as if you were meeting them for the first time? What would you say? What would you tell them?

While the Green Llama is talking, you and Captain Atlas look behind him, and your eyes grow wide in fear. Mrs. Middlebrooks has opened the door and is standing behind the Green Llama!

"Can you explain to the class why you are so late?" asks Mrs. Middlebrooks.

The Green Llama jumps in surprise. **"Oh! Mrs. Middlebrooks! We're so sorry, but we saw aliens when we were coming back from the maze. We tried to help them but . . ."**

Mrs. Middlebrooks abruptly interrupts, **"Didn't I say you could get lost in the maze? Also, what is this about aliens? There is no such thing as aliens!"**

✐ What emotion do you think Mrs. Middlebrooks is feeling? Circle one.

✎ Put the following pictures in the correct sequence of events by numbering them 1 through 5.

Captain Atlas steps forward. **"Pardon me. I didn't mean to cause such a fuss. My robots and I crash-landed on your planet. We're just trying to get back home."**

Mrs. Middlebrooks steps aside to allow everyone into the classroom.

Mrs. Middlebrooks looks at Captain Atlas in disbelief. **"Oh no. Um, my apologies. I had no idea . . . the Green Llama has such an impressive imagination. I wasn't sure if he was letting it get the best of him."**

The Green Llama walks over toward the window. **"I have an idea to help Captain Atlas with his ship. I was telling the captain that everything on Planet 23 is fueled by fruits and vegetables. I'm sure we can use all the fruits and vegetables I've gathered, and with everyone's help, we can get enough to blend and fuel your ship to help you get back home, Captain Atlas."**

"That sounds like a great idea," says Mrs. Middlebrooks. **"Everyone, let's head outside and start to gather as many fruits and veggies as we can."**

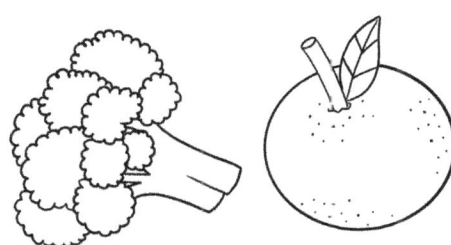

1. How many trees in the garden have fruit growing on them?

_____

2. How many pineapples are growing?

_____

3. How many pieces of fruit are in the basket by the trees?

_____

4. How many groups of different plants are growing in the ground?

_____

5. How many strawberry plants are growing?

_____

✒ Solve the problems to help everyone gather as many fruits and vegetables as they can.

"Look at all that we have gathered!" shouts the Green Llama. "Let's get it all blended up and ready for the ship."

"It's so fascinating how healthy Planet 23 is. I'm sure REP-1 and C3-1 are just about done fixing the spaceship. If we bring this fuel back to the ship, I can finally go home," Captain Atlas says.

You explain to Captain Atlas that he can grow the same healthy fruits and vegetables as you all do on Planet 23. All he has to learn is the word below.

photosynthesis

✎ Plants use this process to turn sunlight into food in their leaves. This is a long word. Trace the dots to spell out the word and then rewrite the word on the lines below.

— — — — — — — — — — — — — —

✎ Read the hints to unscramble the two words that help plants grow.

What comes out every morning that helps us see the world?

HULINTSG

| S | | | L | | G | | T |

FACTS ABOUT OUR SUN

The biggest source of light for our solar system is the sun.

✎ Fill in the blanks with the correct words from the following bank: *old, star, million.*

The sun is the biggest _____ in the center of our solar system.

The surface of the sun is 10 _____ degrees.

The sun is 4.6 billion years _____ .

People and plants need to drink this every day.

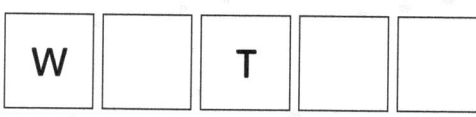
TREWA

| W | | T | | |

Everyone in the class grabs a jug of the blended fruits and vegetables, and they all begin to walk to the spot where the spaceship crashed. REP-1 and C3-1 are just finishing up. The ship is fixed! Hooray!

――――――――――――――――――

✎ Can you make up five sentences using one of the words below in each of your sentences? Write your sentences on the lines.

fuel _____

_____

_____

aliens _____

_____

_____

imagination _____

_____

_____

disbelief _____

_____

_____

impressive _____

_____

_____

Captain Atlas, REP-1, and C3-1 all board the ship. **"The Green Llama taught me so much here on Planet 23! I'll make sure to keep an eye out for a large spaceship! I can't wait to teach everyone back home everything I've learned here! Thanks so much!"** Captain Atlas yells as the ship starts to launch.

Mrs. Middlebrooks and the students wave goodbye to Captain Atlas. As the spaceship shoots back into the sky, she looks around and asks, **"Has anyone seen the Green Llama and his new friend?"**

Captain Atlas looks over at M.A.T. **"The Green Llama was right. That was the coolest planet I've ever seen!"**

The Green Llama peeks his head out from inside the spaceship and says . . .

HOPE YOU'RE READY FOR THE NEXT ADVENTURE!

Color in the page and wave goodbye!

ALL ABOUT YOU

Can you start your own garden? What kind of materials and supplies would you need to get your garden started? What would you grow in your garden? Why?

_____

_____

_____

THINK ABOUT THE STORY

Fruits and vegetables really helped Captain Atlas's spaceship. How can you help people in your community eat more fruits and vegetables? What would you tell them? Can you draw a sign for people to read about fruits and vegetables?

_____

_____

Mrs. Middlebrooks is a very good teacher. What are things good teachers do? Who is your favorite teacher? Why?

_____

_____

ACTIVITY

What does the word "expression" mean? Can you express yourself without words? If you met somebody that did not speak the same language as you, how would you communicate? Think of an activity where you need to communicate certain information to other students without making sounds.

THE END

The Green Llama

The Green Llama would like to thank all the teachers, parents, and especially YOU! None of this would be possible without your continued support!

Until next time . . . gotta blast!

Today is the beginning
of a friendship forever.

Even when we part ways,
know that I'm by your side
if you need me whenever.